Rhymes With . . .

Read each animal name. Write the rhyming word from the box.
Then think of and write another word that rhymes with it.

| honey | break | snow | eye | tail | word | note | me | chair |

1. bee

2. doe

3. bunny

4. whale

5. snake

6. bear

7. goat

8. bird

9. fly

Rhyme Time

Fill in the circles next to the three rhyming words in each group.

The Tortoise and the Hare

Read each sentence. Write the word from the box that means the same as the word or words in **pink** print.

animals	plods	story	message
reached	start	noisy	sleep

1. "The Tortoise and the Hare" is an old **tale**.

2. In it, the two very different **creatures** race each other.

3. The hare quickly hops off at the **beginning** of the race.

4. The tortoise **slowly moves** along.

5. Since he is so far ahead, the hare decides to eat and **nap**.

6. After awhile, the hare wakes up to **loud** cheers.

7. The tortoise has **arrived at** the Finish Line.

8. The **moral** of the story is *Slow and steady wins the race.*

The Book Swap

Read each sentence. Write the word from the box that means the opposite of the word in **red** print.

wonderful	find	make	Children
Everybody	end	above	oldest

1. At the **beginning** of the year our school holds a Book Swap.

2. **Nobody** brings in books from home he or she wants to trade.

3. The **youngest** students collect and sort the books.

4. The third and fourth graders **destroy** flyers and invitations.

5. The second graders make signs to put **below** the books.

6. When the Book Swap begins, kids **lose** the books they want.

7. **Adults** pay with coupons they got for bringing in books.

8. The Book Swap is a **terrible** way to get new books for summer.

Be Quiet, Bee!

Write each word in the *right* blank.

be
bee

blew
blue

to
two

hole
whole

wood
would

eye
I

aunt
ant

buy
by

1. If you will __________ still, the __________ won't bother you.

2. The wind __________ off Jason's __________ hat.

3. Marta gave __________ flowers __________ her teacher.

4. The __________ mouse family crawled in its __________.

5. Kelsey __________ like some __________ for the campfire.

6. __________ have something in my __________.

7. Brad's __________ is watching a little red __________.

8. Amanda walked __________ the park on her way to __________ ice cream.

We All Fall Down

Some words, like *fall*, have more than one meaning.

> **fall** 1. to come down from a higher place; drop
> 2. season of the year; autumn
> 3. waterfall (usually written as a plural—*falls*)

Read each sentence. Decide if the word *fall* or *falls* matches the first, second, or third meaning. Write **1**, **2**, or **3** in the circle.

○ "Ashes, ashes, we all **fall** down."

○ Leaves change color in the **fall**.

○ If you **fall** on the mat, you won't get hurt.

○ They went over the **falls** in their raft.

○ Whenever the baby **falls**, she laughs and says "Boom!"

○ My favorite time of the year is **fall**.

○ If you stand close to the **falls**, the water will spray you.

○ If enough snow **falls**, we can go sledding tomorrow.

○ You need to wear a sweatshirt on cool **fall** days.

○ If you **fall** out of that tree, you'll break a leg.

Compound Word Fun

Write the word from the box that will make each set of compound words.

light	water	sun	boat	cake	butter	ball	tooth

__________ cup
__________ fly
__________ milk

__________ paste
__________ brush
__________ pick

foot __________
basket __________
base __________

row __________
sail __________
tug __________

__________ rise
__________ flower
__________ shine

__________ fall
__________ color
__________ melon

pan __________
cup __________
fruit __________

head __________
flash __________
moon __________

"Not" Words

The prefixes *un-*, *im-*, and *in-* mean "not."
Draw a line to match each word to its picture.

Dancer—One Who Dances

The suffixes *-er* and *-or* mean "one who." Write each word from the box under the matching picture. Circle the suffix.

| painter | actor | farmer | sculptor | dancer |
| doctor | teacher | author | plumber | |

dancer

Diego Rivera

Use words from the box to finish each sentence.

pictures	painted	artist	grew	born
working	Mexico	huge	walls	asked

1. Diego Rivera was a famous __________.

2. He was __________ on December 8, 1886.

3. He lived in __________.

4. When he was a child, he was always drawing __________.

5. He drew everywhere—even on the __________!

6. As Diego __________ older, he liked to paint pictures of real people

   and the things they did.

7. Diego Rivera painted __________ pictures called murals.

8. He __________ them on walls of schools, palaces, and other

   buildings for everyone to see.

9. Diego Rivera was __________ to paint murals in San

   Francisco, Detroit, and New York City.

10. Diego Rivera was still __________ when he died at age 70.

Wrinkled Fingers

Read the paragraph. Answer the questions.

Have you ever noticed that your fingers get wrinkled when you take a bath? Your body is covered with layers of skin. There is a thin coat of oil on your skin that keeps water out. Soapy bath water takes away the oil. Then water seeps into your skin and makes the wrinkles.

1. What covers your skin and keeps water out?

2. What makes your fingers wrinkle?

3. What do you think the word *seeps* means?

4. Do you think your body makes new oil once you are out of the bath? Explain why or why not.

Caribou

Read the paragraph. Answer the questions.

Caribou (CARE uh boo) are a kind of deer. They live in the cold northern areas of North America. Caribou and reindeer are the only kinds of deer whose males and females both have antlers. Caribou travel in large groups called herds. There are sometimes 10,000 caribou in the herd.

1. What is a caribou?

2. Where do caribou live?

3. How are caribou like reindeer?

4. What is the most interesting thing you learned about caribou? Explain why.

Way Down South

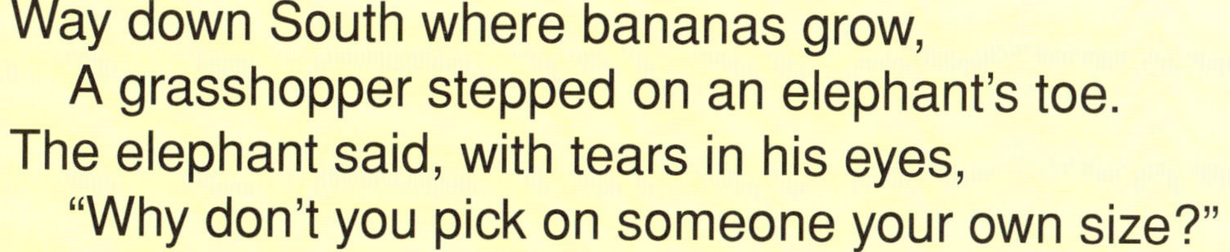

Read the poem. Answer the questions.

> Way down South where bananas grow,
>   A grasshopper stepped on an elephant's toe.
> The elephant said, with tears in his eyes,
>   "Why don't you pick on someone your own size?"
>
>   —*Anonymous*

1. Is this a silly poem or a serious one?

2. What is something in this poem that might really happen?

3. What are two things that wouldn't really happen?

4. Sometimes in a poem, words at the end of a line rhyme.
   Write the rhyming word pairs in this poem.

Headlines

A headline tells the main idea of a news story.

Read these stories. Choose the best headline from the box for each story. Write it above the story.

Headlines

Good Fairy to Visit Town
Woman Dies From Eating Many Animals
Pesky Fly Is Missing
Mice Are Having a Bad Day
Naughty Rabbit Turned Into Goon

An old woman who accidentally swallowed a fly, died from eating several other animals. Her family said she ate a spider, bird, cat, dog, goat, cow, and horse in that order to catch the fly. The horse, of course, was too much.

A naughty rabbit named Little Bunny Foo Foo was turned into a goon yesterday. He was bothering field mice all day long. The Good Fairy gave Foo three chances, but he wouldn't stop. So she changed him from a rabbit to a goon.

Animal Names

Read this chart to answer the questions.

Animal	Female	Male	Baby
deer	doe	buck	fawn
elephant	cow	bull	calf
horse	mare	stallion	foal
kangaroo	doe	buck	joey
lion	lioness	lion	cub
sheep	ewe	ram	lamb
whale	cow	bull	calf
zebra	mare	stallion	colt

A. What is a baby deer called? _______________________________________

B. What is a female lion called? _____________________________________

C. What is a *ram*? ____

D. What is a *joey*? ____

E. Which two animals are called *cow, bull,* and *calf*?

____

F. For which two animals is a female called a *doe*?

____

G. Which of these animals have you seen? (include names)_______________

____

____

All About Flying

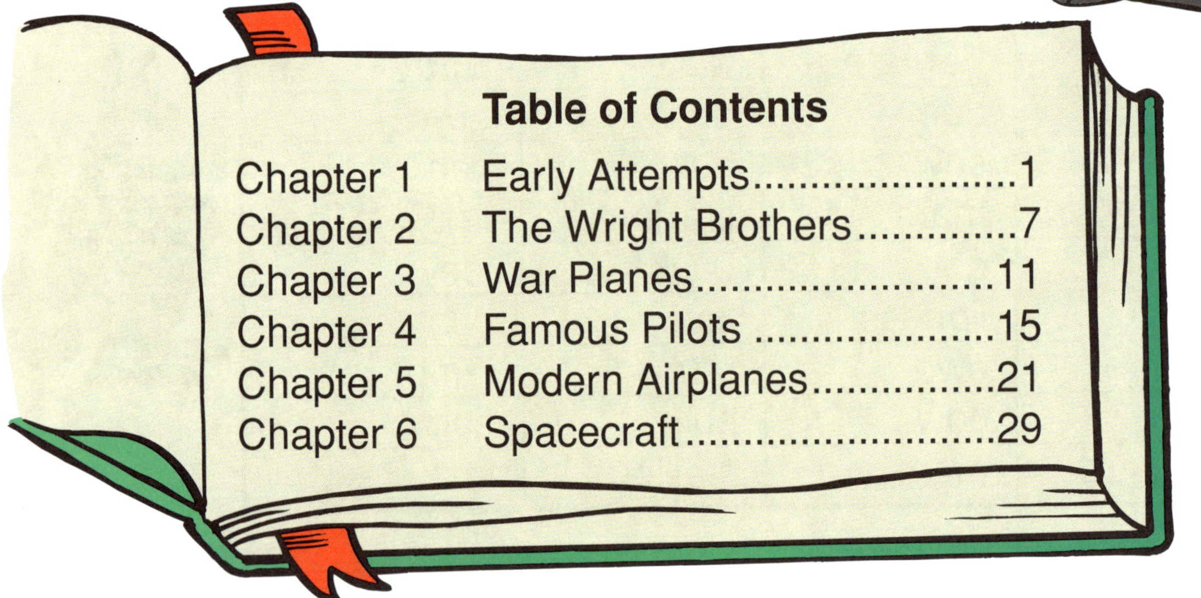

Read this table of contents. Then answer the questions.

Table of Contents

A. Which chapter tells about the Wright Brothers?________

B. On what page does the Famous Pilots chapter begin?________

C. If you are on page 11, what are you reading about?________________

____

D. If you want to find out about planes you might fly in today, what is the

name of the chapter you should read?________________

____

E. If you want to find out about the space shuttle or rockets, which

chapter should you read? ________________

F. If you are on page 4, what are you reading about?________________

____

Long or Short?

Read the words in each box. Decide if the word has a short or long vowel.
Write the word on the correct pencil.

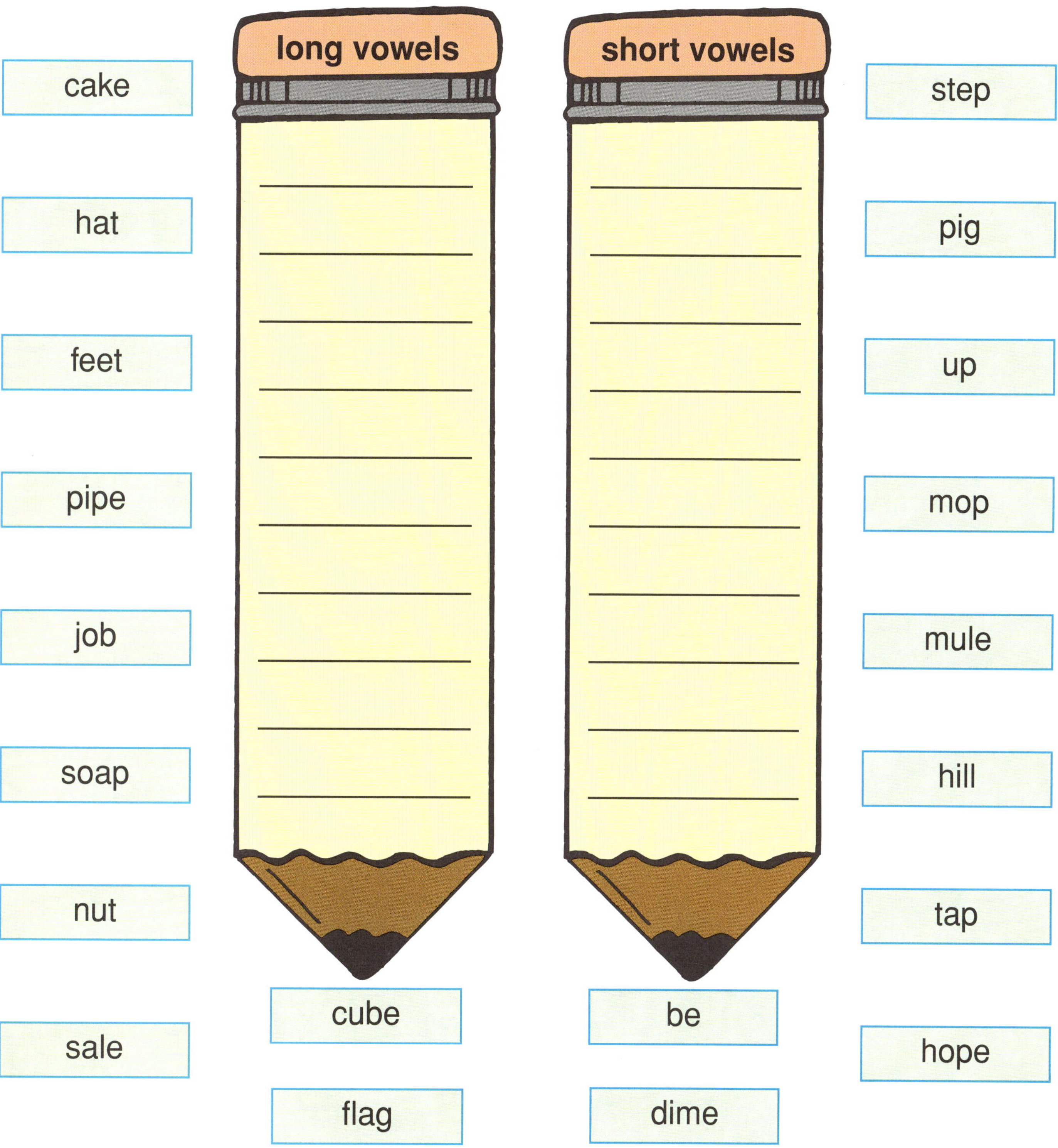

Something's Fishy

Write the vowels **a, e, i , o,** or **u** to complete each word and color.

long vowels = orange   short vowels = blue

Which Word?

Write the answers on the lines. Use the words in the box.

forty	March	purple	girl	skirt	circus
market	perfume	fern	nurse	birthday	farm

1. Which word is the name of a month? _________________

2. Which word is a number? _________________

3. Which word names a color? _________________

4. Which word is something that smells good? _________________

5. Which word is a green plant? _________________

6. Which word is someone who works in a hospital? _________________

7. Which word is the opposite of *boy*? _________________

8. Which word is a place where corn grows? _________________

9. Which word is a place with clowns? _________________

10. Which word is a day to celebrate? _________________

11. Which word is a place to buy things? _________________

12. Which word is something to wear? _________________

Book or Boot?

Read each word below. Decide if the word has the **oo** sound as in **book** or the **oo** sound as in **boot**. Write the words in the correct box.

tool
took
moon
school
hook
room
good
foot
tooth
hood
roof
cook
soon
wood
pool
stood
shook
look
mood
zoo

book

_____________ _____________

_____________ _____________

_____________ _____________

_____________ _____________

_____________ _____________

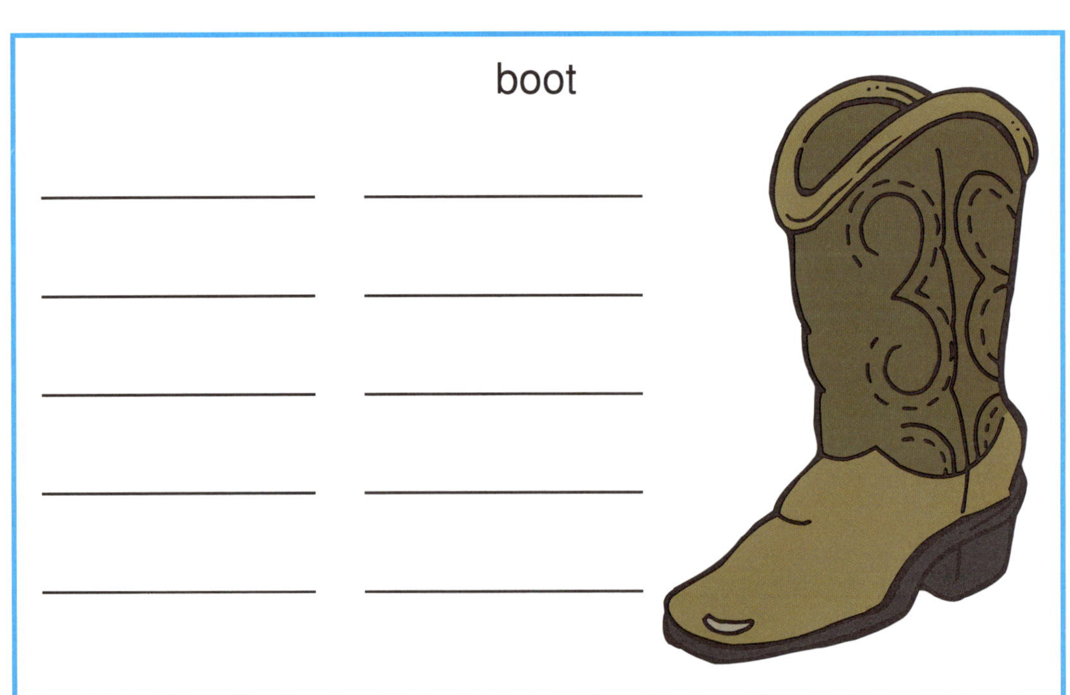

boot

_____________ _____________

_____________ _____________

_____________ _____________

_____________ _____________

_____________ _____________

Cow or Crow?

Read each word below. Decide if the word has the **ow** sound as in **crow** or the **ow** sound as in **cow**. Write the word on the correct list.

town	grow
clown	know
owl	blow
slow	flower
window	brown
snow	now
show	how
bowl	down
tow	shower
towel	below
throw	crown
power	glow

cow

crow

Fun With Riddles

Read each riddle. Find the answer in the word box and write it on the line.

1. You can plant a seed in me. I will help it grow.

   What am I?

   ____

2. I am the sound that comes out of your mouth when you speak.

   What am I?

   ____

3. I am the opposite of a girl.

   What am I?

   ____

4. You can play with me. I can be a ball, a kite, or a doll.

   What am I?

   ____

5. You can buy things with me. I am made of metal.

   What am I?

   ____

6. I am the sharp end on a pencil.

   What am I?

   ____

Write your own riddles for these words.

7. noise ____

   ____

8. boil ____

   ____

Space Is the Place

Number each group of words in alphabetical order.

A.
___ Jupiter
___ gravity
___ galaxy

B.
___ Uranus
___ Neptune
___ universe

C.
___ Mercury
___ moon
___ meteor

D.
___ Saturn
___ satellite
___ Sun

E.
___ rings
___ rocket
___ rotate

F.
___ crater
___ comet
___ spins

G.
___ Earth
___ eclipse
___ energy

H.
___ star
___ system
___ solar

I.
___ ocean
___ Orion
___ orbit

J.
___ planet
___ phase
___ Pluto

K.
___ astronaut
___ air
___ Apollo

L.
___ space
___ Sputnik
___ shuttle

Let's Ride!

Write the contraction for each pair of words. Take out the boldfaced letters. Put in an apostrophe. Example: should + n**o**t = shouldn't

1.

2.

3.

4.

5.

6.

7.

8.

9.

Who's Fishing?

Fill in the circle next to the two words that make each contraction.

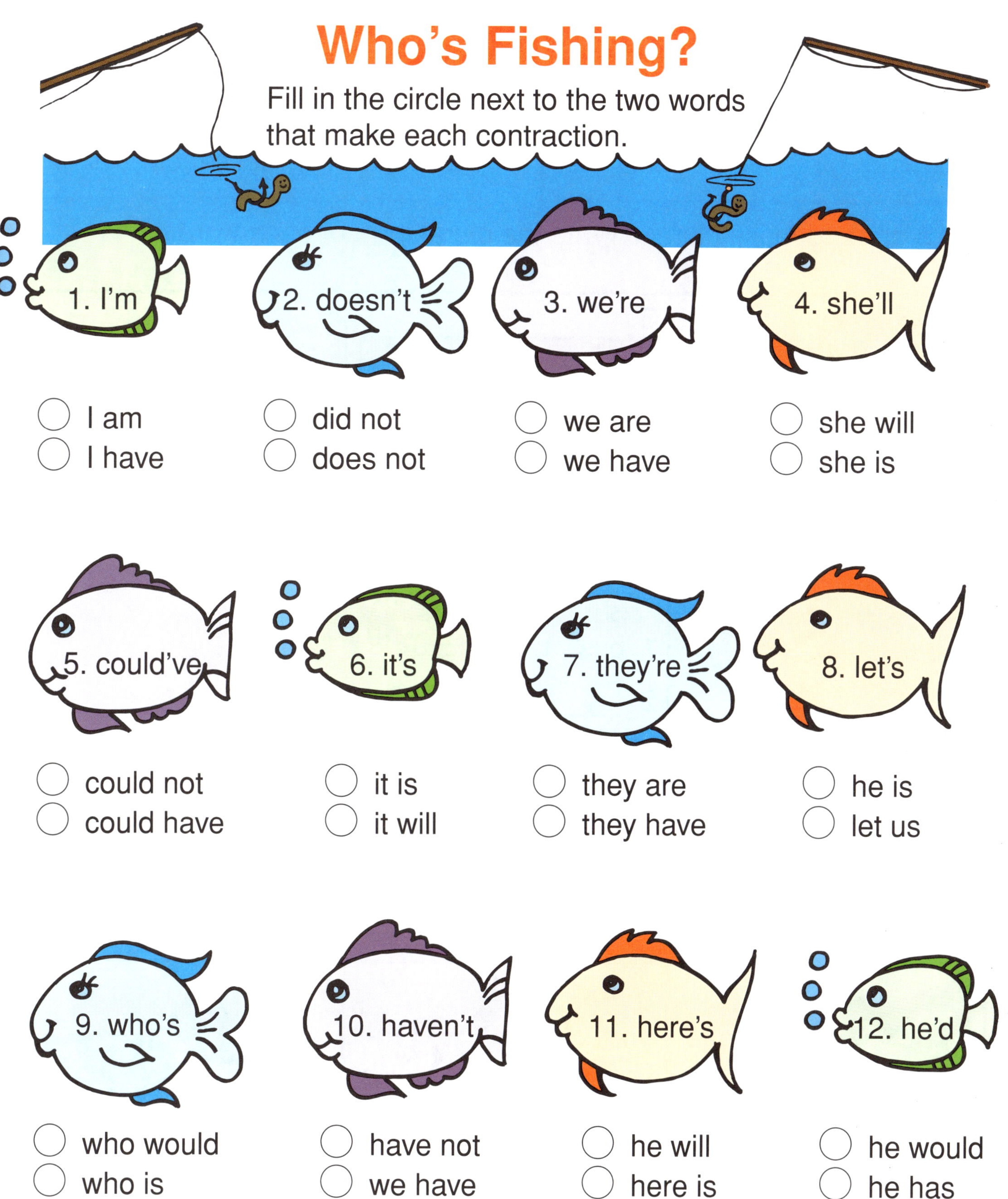

1. ○ I am
   ○ I have

2. ○ did not
   ○ does not

3. ○ we are
   ○ we have

4. ○ she will
   ○ she is

5. ○ could not
   ○ could have

6. ○ it is
   ○ it will

7. ○ they are
   ○ they have

8. ○ he is
   ○ let us

9. ○ who would
   ○ who is

10. ○ have not
    ○ we have

11. ○ he will
    ○ here is

12. ○ he would
    ○ he has

More Than One

Add **s** to most words to make plurals.

Add **es** to words that end in **sh, ch, s,** or **x** to make them plural.

Add **s** or **es** to make plurals. Write the plural form of each word.

A.	B.	C.
1 house	1 inch	1 shell
2 _ _ _ _ _ _ _	2 _ _ _ _ _ _	2 _ _ _ _ _ _
D.	E.	F.
1 box	1 bus	1 line
2 _ _ _ _ _	2 _ _ _ _ _	2 _ _ _ _ _
G.	H.	I.
1 pen	1 chair	1 bush
2 _ _ _ _ _	2 _ _ _ _ _ _	2 _ _ _ _ _ _
J.	K.	L.
1 key	1 fox	1 dish
2 _ _ _ _ _	2 _ _ _ _ _	2 _ _ _ _ _ _

Late Last Night

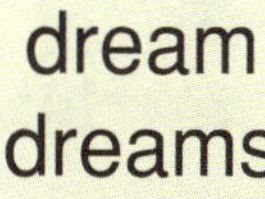

Choose the correct word from each box. Write it on the line.

dream dreams	1. Last night I had a strange _______________.
alien aliens	2. Two _______________ knocked on my window.
bed beds	3. I sat up in my _______________ and looked.

eye eyes	4. One alien had three _______________ and four ears.
ear ears	5. The other had six eyes and one _______________.
noise noises	6. They made a strange _______________, then left.
stair stairs	7. I raced down the _______________ and ran outside.

answer answers	8. I called "Hello!" but there was no _______________.
light lights	9. Then I saw a bunch of flashing _______________ in the sky. Their spaceship flew away.

Present and Past

Draw lines to match up the present tense
and past tense verbs.

Today you . . .	Yesterday you . . .	Today you . . .	Yesterday you . . .
play	went	see	lived
work	liked	get	saw
go	swam	take	knew
like	played	live	got
swim	worked	know	took
fly	called	give	thought
talk	sang	think	gave
sing	flew	tell	wanted
call	talked	come	put
are	wrote	want	told
write	were	show	came
have	made	put	asked
make	did	read	showed
say	said	ask	tried
do	had	try	read

Past or Present?

Write the correct verb from the box to finish this poem.

| clopped |
| clops |

Yesterday the horse clip-_____________,

    Now it _____________ some more.

| hops |
| hopped |

Yesterday the rabbit _____________,

    Now it _____________ some more.

| creeps |
| crept |

Yesterday the turtle _____________,

    Now it _____________ some more.

| leapt |
| leaps |

Yesterday the bullfrog _____________,

    Now it _____________ some more.

| stalks |
| stalked |

Yesterday the sly cat _____________,

    Now it _____________ some more.

| squawked |
| squawks |

Yesterday the blackbird _____________,

    Now it _____________ no more!

My New Pet

Circle the word in each sentence that should begin with a capital letter. Write it correctly on the blank.

_______________ 1. My birthday was in september.

_______________ 2. My Grandpa rogers got me a pet.

_______________ 3. it was a little black kitten.

_______________ 4. First, I named her midnight.

_______________ 5. But the kitten liked to scratch a lot so i renamed her Captain Hook.

_______________ 6. Last tuesday we took Captain Hook to the veterinarian.

_______________ 7. Our veterinarian is dr. Hayes.

_______________ 8. Dr. hayes gave Captain Hook the shots she needed.

_______________ 9. she did not like it at all!

_______________ 10. Captain hook is happy to be home with me now.

You Name It

Fill in the blanks with names of people, places, or dates. Remember to begin each with a capital letter.

1. My full name is _______________________

2. I was born in the month of _______________________

3. A good friend of mine is _______________________

4. The name of my town or city is _______________________

5. The name of my country is _______________________

6. A place I would like to visit is _______________________

7. The leader of my country is _______________________

8. A person I admire is _______________________

The Taj Mahal

Write the words in the right order to make sentences. Make sure each sentence begins with a capital letter and ends with a period.

1. Taj Mahal   famous   The   building   is   a

2. is   India   in   It

3. Taj Mahal   The   many   years   ago   was   built

4. built   to   honor   It   was   a   queen   who   died

The Manatee

Write the words in the right order to
make sentences. Make sure each
sentence begins with a capital letter
and ends with a period.

1. manatee   mammal   The   is   a

2. water   lives   in   It

3. Manatees   reasons   for   two   are   endangered

4. water   Their   polluted   is

5. manatees   run   over   Motorboats   kill   them   and

Totem Pole

Read each sentence.
Write a **.** at the end if it is a telling sentence.
Write a **?** at the end if it is a question.
Write a **!** at the end if it shows strong feelings.

1. Wow, that's a beautiful totem pole

2. Have you ever seen a totem pole

3. It is a tall pole carved from a log

4. Do you know what totem poles are for

5. Some totem poles tell a story or legend

6. Others are carved to honor someone

7. Who makes totem poles

8. They are carved by Native Americans of the Northwest Coast

9. The Tsimshian tribe carve totem poles

10. Where do the Tsimshian people live

11. They live in British Columbia, Canada

12. I wish I could carve a totem pole

Goodbye, Cassie!

Read each sentence.
Write a **.** at the end if it is a telling sentence.
Write a **?** at the end if it is a question.
Write a **!** at the end if it shows strong feelings.

1. Oh, no

2. My best friend, Cassie, is moving away

3. She and I have been friends since we were babies

4. Have you ever had a friend move away

5. What am I going to do

6. My parents are having a party tonight for Cassie's family

7. We may get to stay up until midnight

8. Tomorrow the moving van comes

9. How long will it take to load up their things

10. Cassie said she will write me letters

11. I can visit her next summer

12. I'll miss you, Cassie

The First Phone

Circle the 10 words that are spelled wrong. Write each correctly on the line. Check your spellings with the words in the box.

1. _______________

2. _______________

3. _______________

4. _______________

5. _______________

6. _______________

7. _______________

8. _______________

9. _______________

10. _______________

Do yoo know who invented the telephone? It wuz Alexander Graham Bell. He did it over a hundred yeers ago.

Thomas Watson helpt him. He was wating in another room to heer Bell's message. The first words Bell spoke on the fone were: "Mr. Watson, come here. I wunt you." Alexander Graham Bell sed those words because he had just spilld something on himself!

hear	helped	phone	said	spilled	waiting	want	was	years	you

Finally!

Circle the 10 words that are spelled wrong. Write each correctly on the line. Check your spellings with the words in the box.

1. _______________
2. _______________
3. _______________
4. _______________
5. _______________
6. _______________
7. _______________
8. _______________
9. _______________
10. _______________

I just lost mi first baby tooth! It took a long time. Everybody I kno lost a tooth in kindergarten or ferst grad. But it took me until second grade.

My parents took me to the dentist last yeer. The dentist told me not to woory. She said my baby teeth would fall out when my uther teeth were reddy to come in.

And wun did. Finally! I wonder whut the Tooth Fairy will bring me?

| first | grade | know | my | one | other | ready | what | worry | year |

You Are Invited to . . .
What would you like to be invited to? Design and write an invitation you would like to receive.

Thank You!

Think of someone who has done something for you. Write him or her a thank-you note. Decorate the card with pictures that match.

Thank you!

Dear Eagle

If you could be any animal, which would you be? Write a friendly letter to that animal. Choose one of these topics to write about:

- [ ] why you like that animal
- [ ] what you want to learn about that animal
- [ ] how you are different from that animal

Down by the Bay

Have you ever sung "Down by the Bay"? Make up your own rhyming verses to replace the words in *slanted letters.*

Down by the bay, where the watermelons grow,
Back to my home, I dare not go.
For if I do, my mother will say:
Did you ever see *a bear*
combing its hair,
Down by the bay?

1

Did you ever see ___________________

___________________ ,

Down by the bay?

2

Did you ever see ___________________

___________________ ,

Down by the bay?

3

Did you ever see ___________________

___________________ ,

Down by the bay?

4

Did you ever see ___________________

___________________ ,

Down by the bay?

Turtles

Read these notes about turtles.
Write complete sentences using the ideas from the notes.

Turtle Notes

General
- reptiles
- cold-blooded
- hatch from eggs
- most eat both
  plants and animals

Body
- hard shell
- four legs
- tail
- hard beak

Some kinds
- pond turtles
- snapping turtles
- mud turtles
- sea turtles
- tortoises

Sample: <u>Turtles are cold-blooded animals.</u>

1. ____

____

2. ____

____

3. ____

____

4. ____

____

Kitten in a Tree

A paragraph is a group of sentences about the same topic.
The sentences in a paragraph should be in order.

Write **1, 2, 3,** and **4** to show the order in which
these sentences should appear in a paragraph.

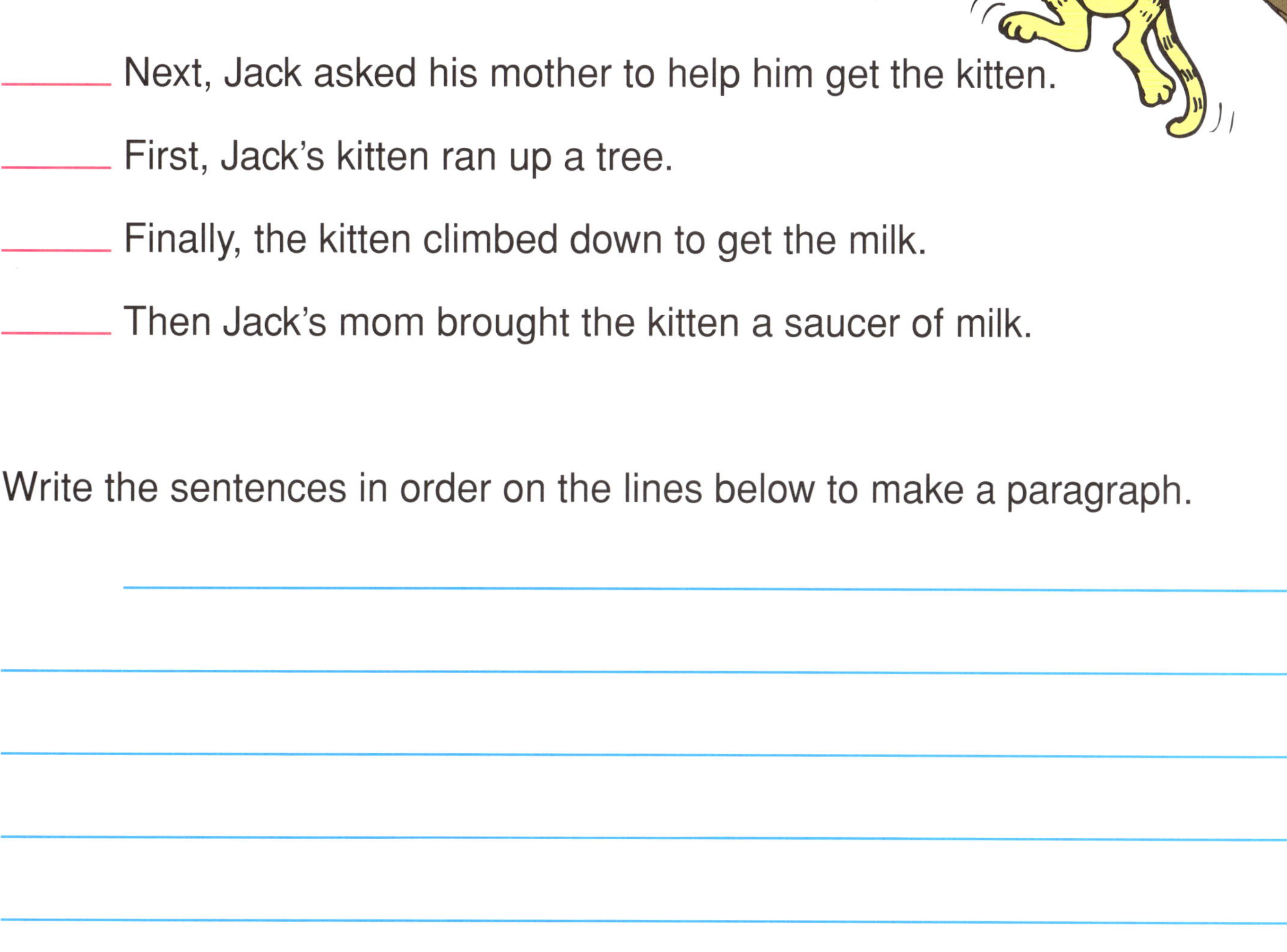

_______ Next, Jack asked his mother to help him get the kitten.

_______ First, Jack's kitten ran up a tree.

_______ Finally, the kitten climbed down to get the milk.

_______ Then Jack's mom brought the kitten a saucer of milk.

Write the sentences in order on the lines below to make a paragraph.

Imagine That!

Imagine that you have been selected to be the teacher for your class for one day.

How do you feel?
What will you do?
What will you have the students do?
Do you think you'll like being the teacher?

Write your ideas into a paragraph on the lines below.

Teacher for a Day

What Will You Do?

Read the sentences below. Tell how you would solve each problem.

You found a five-dollar bill on your way home from school.
What will you do?

You see someone picking on one of your friends.
What will you do?

Which Group?

Write the words in the correct groups.
Then write one more word for each group.

basketball	skin
ladybug	soccer
grasshopper	black
purple	brain
ant	stomach
gold	ice skating
green	swimming
bones	butterfly

Insects

Sports

Colors

Body Parts

What a Group!

Write the name of each group in the box.
Write one more word for each group.

1.	**2.**	**3.**
whale sea horse starfish ___________	pine oak maple ___________	piano drums trumpet ___________
4.	**5.**	**6.**
Earth Saturn Neptune ___________	yogurt cheese ice cream ___________	lettuce cucumber corn ___________
7.	**8.**	**9.**
one hundred eight fourteen ___________	apple banana pear ___________	markers paintbrush yarn ___________

Word Analogies

Think about whether the words being compared mean the same or the opposite. Write the missing word.

| right | noisy | angry | sleepy | begin | woman | below | less | go |

Large is to **big** as

tired is to

_____sleepy_____.

Yes is to **no** as

stop is to

_____________.

Boy is to **girl** as

man is to

_____________.

Tiny is to **small** as

mad is to

_____________.

Day is to **night** as

wrong is to

_____________.

Finish is to **end** as

start is to

_____________.

Fast is to **slow** as

quiet is to

_____________.

Shut is to **close** as

under is to

_____________.

Old is to **young** as

more is to

_____________.

Pencil Is to Write As . . .

Think about how the words are being compared.
Write the missing word from the pencil.

Part to Whole—the first word names part
of the thing named by the second word
finger is to *hand* as *toe* is to *foot*

Object to Action—the second word tells
what the first word does
fish is to *swim* as *bird* is to *fly*

---

1. **Mouth** is to **speak** as **ear** is to _________________ .

2. **Paw** is to **bear** as **flipper** is to _________________ .

3. **Tree** is to **forest** as **cactus** is to _________________ .

4. **Pencil** is to **write** as **crayon** is to _________________ .

5. **Dog** is to **bark** as **cat** is to _________________ .

6. **Minute** is to **hour** as **month** is to _________________ .

7. **Wheelchair** is to **roll** as **pogo stick** is to _________________ .

8. **Heart** is to **body** as **engine** is to _________________ .

9. **Chapter** is to **book** as **verse** is to _________________ .

10. **Fire** is to **burn** as **ice** is to _________________ .

What a Change!

A butterfly and a frog change a lot as they grow from an egg to an adult.
Number the stages of their life from **1** to **4**.

Butterfly

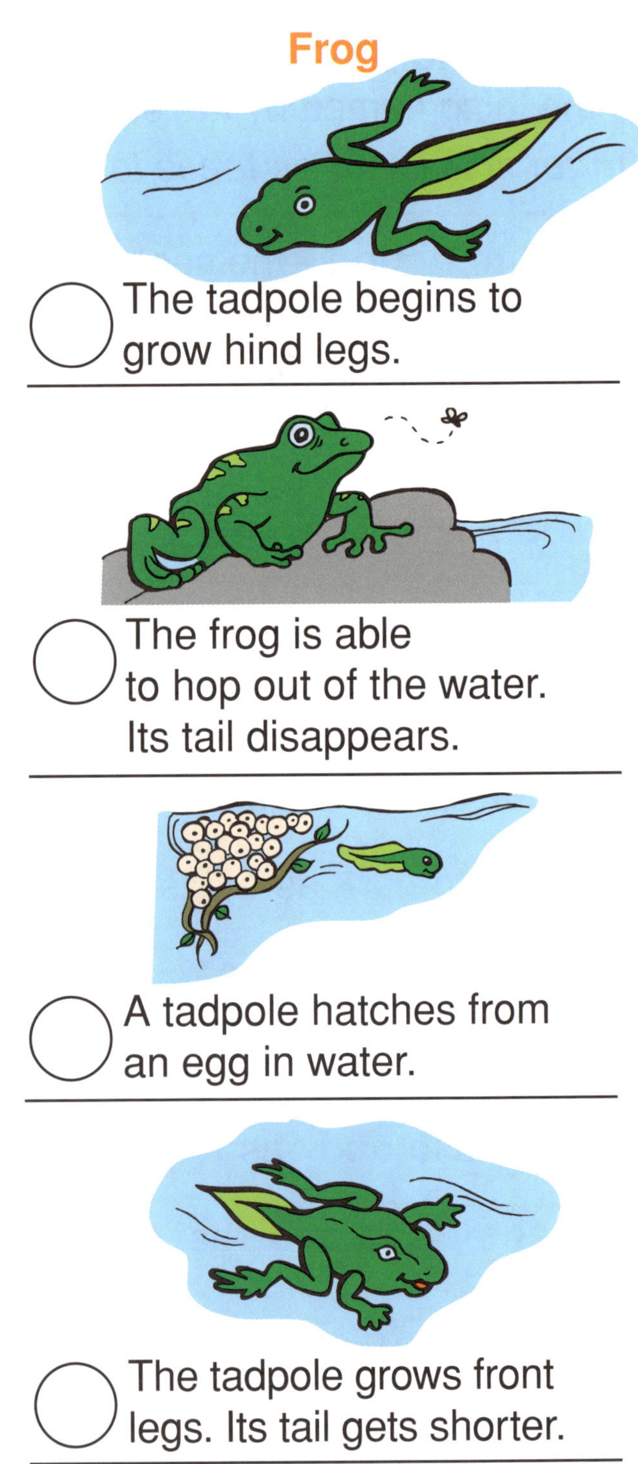

◯ The caterpillar makes a silky case around itself called a chrysalis.

◯ A caterpillar hatches from an egg.

◯ The caterpillar eats and grows bigger.

◯ A butterfly comes out of the chrysalis.

Frog

◯ The tadpole begins to grow hind legs.

◯ The frog is able to hop out of the water. Its tail disappears.

◯ A tadpole hatches from an egg in water.

◯ The tadpole grows front legs. Its tail gets shorter.

An Art Project

Read the directions for this art project.
Number the steps from **1** to **6** inside the circles.

◯ Keep adding tissue-paper pieces and painting them until the picture is done. Let it dry overnight.

◯ Gather what you need: white paper, colored tissue paper, liquid starch, pencil, and paintbrush.

◯ Draw a simple picture on the white paper.

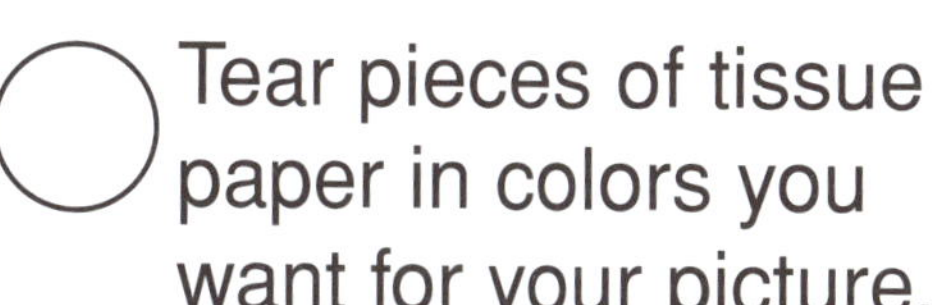

◯ Tear pieces of tissue paper in colors you want for your picture.

◯ Put tissue-paper pieces on the picture.

◯ Paint over the pieces with liquid starch.

What Might Happen?

A **cause** is the reason something happens.
An **effect** is the thing that happens.
Read each cause sentence. Write an effect sentence.

Cause: A big wave hit Alma's sand castle.

Effect: __________________________

____

____

Cause: Three feet of snow fell in a snowstorm last night.

Effect: __________________________

____

____

Cause: Friendship School has a new computer lab.

Effect: __________________________

____

____

Cause: Tony practices the piano 20 minutes every day.

Effect: __________________________

____

____

Think About It

Read each sentence and look at the picture.
Fill in the circles beside the two sentences that could match it.

1. Kevin doesn't want to eat lunch.

   ◯ He is hungry.
   ◯ He is full.
   ◯ He doesn't feel well.

2. Holly is swinging really high and screaming.

   ◯ She's scared.
   ◯ She's tired.
   ◯ She's having a good time.

3. You go to school and find you have a substitute teacher.

   ◯ Your teacher is sick.
   ◯ Your teacher is noisy.
   ◯ Your teacher is at a day-long meeting.

4. Your little brother is crying.

   ◯ He is hurt.
   ◯ He is sad.
   ◯ He is bored.

Picture Clues

Look at each picture. Read the sentence. Fill in the circle beside *true* if the sentence is true. Fill in the circle beside *can't tell* if you can't tell for sure by looking at the picture. Then explain your answer.

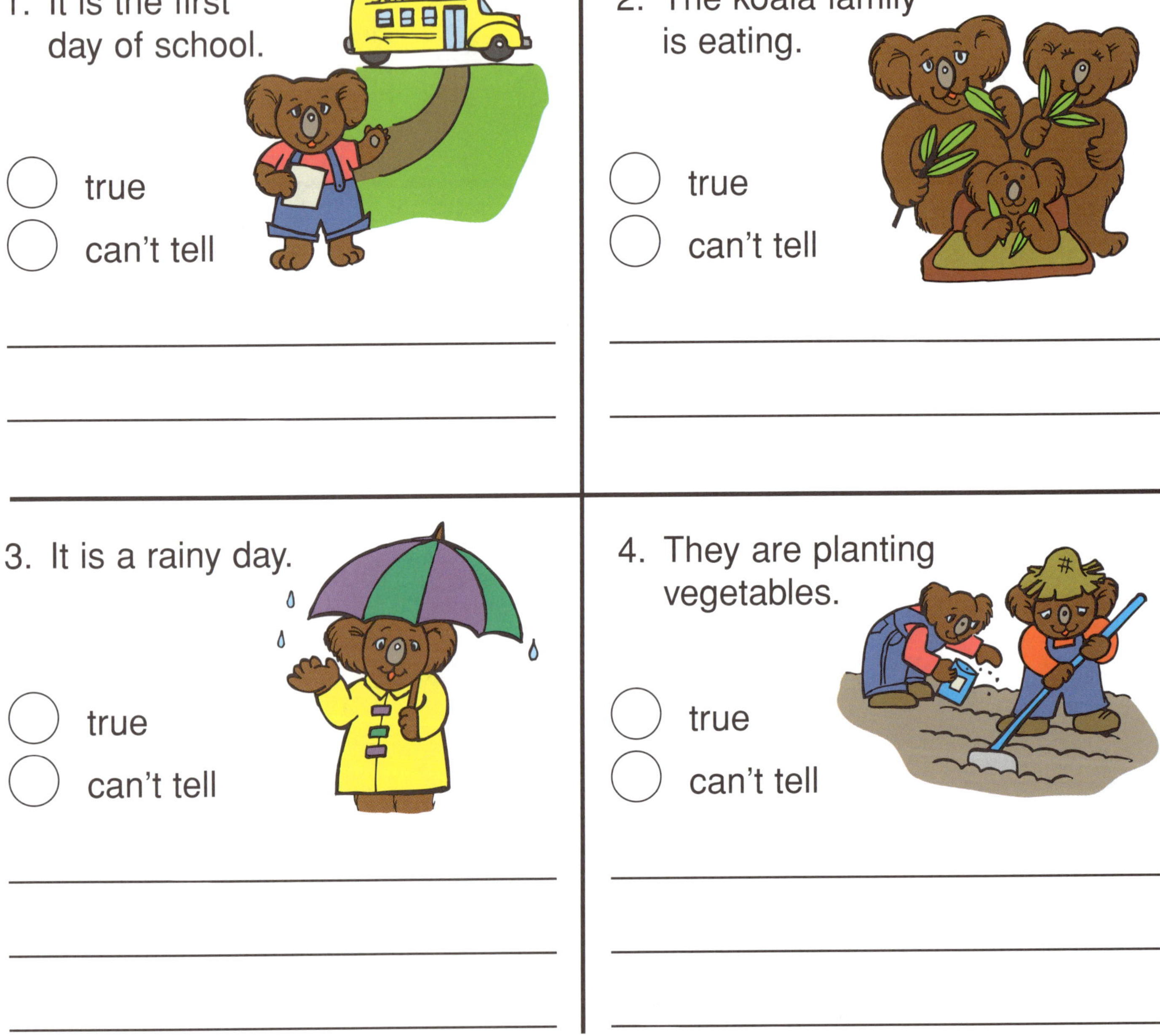

1. It is the first day of school.

○ true
○ can't tell

____

____

2. The koala family is eating.

○ true
○ can't tell

____

____

3. It is a rainy day.

○ true
○ can't tell

____

____

4. They are planting vegetables.

○ true
○ can't tell

____

____

A Good Friend

What makes someone a good friend? Think of four ideas and write them in the chart. Then grade yourself. Write your name beside the star. Read your ideas. Decide how often you act that way and mark an **X** in the matching box.

⭐	Always	Usually	Sometimes	Never
1. __________________ __________________ __________________				
2. __________________ __________________ __________________				
3. __________________ __________________ __________________				
4. __________________ __________________ __________________				

What's Missing?

Find the pattern.
Fill in the missing numbers.

A. 75, 74, 73, _____, 71, _____, _____, 68, _____, _____, _____, _____

B. 215, 216, 217, _____, 219, _____, 221, _____, _____, 224

C. 25, 30, 35, _____, _____, 50, _____, _____, 65, _____, _____, 80

D. 1,000, 900, 800, 700, _____, 500, _____, _____, _____, 100

E. 2, 4, 6, _____, 10, _____, _____, _____, 18, _____, _____, _____, 26

F. 99, 97, 95, _____, 91, 89, _____, _____, _____, 81, _____, 77, _____

G. 540, 550, 560, _____, _____, 590, 600, _____, 620, _____

H. 3, 6, 9, 12, _____, 18, _____, 24, _____, _____, 33, _____, 39, _____

I. 11, 21, 31, 41, _____, _____, _____, 81, _____, 101, _____, 121

J. 800, 750, 700, 650, _____, 550, 500, _____, 400, _____, 300

K. 100, 95, 90, _____, 80, _____, _____, 65, _____, _____, _____, 45

L. 9, 10, 19, 20, 29, 30, _____, 40, 49, _____, 59, _____, _____, 70

Patterns

Find the pattern.
Write the missing numbers.

A. 83, 84, 85, _____, 87, _____, _____, _____, 91, _____, _____, 94

B. 346, 345, 344, _____, 342, _____, 340, _____, 338, _____

C. 20, 30, 40, _____, 60, _____, _____, 90, _____, 110, 120, _____

D. 100, 95, 90, _____, 80, 75, _____, _____, 60, _____, _____, _____

E. 100, 200, 300, _____, 500, _____, _____, 800, _____, 1,000

F. 58, 56, 54, _____, 50, _____, 46, _____, _____, _____, 38, _____, 34

G. 300, 305, 310, _____, 320, 325, _____, _____, 340, _____

H. 740, 730, 720, _____, 700, _____, 680, 670, _____, 650, 640

I. 1, 3, 5, _____, 9, _____, _____, 15, _____, 19, _____, 23, 25, _____

J. 100, 102, 104, 106, _____, 110, _____, 114, _____, _____

K. 999, 899, 799, _____, 599, _____, _____, 299, _____, 99

L. 4, 8, 12, 16, _____, 24, 28, _____, 36, _____, 44, 48, 52, _____, 60

More, Less, and Equal

49 > 36 49 is greater than 36	54 < 88 54 is less than 88	48 = 48 48 is equal to 48

Rearrange each set of numbers to solve the math sentences.

A. 

3 1 > 2 4
2 3 < 4 1

B. 

__ __ > __ __
__ __ < __ __

C. 

__ __ > __ __
__ __ < __ __

D. 

__ __ > __ __
__ __ < __ __
__ __ = __ __

E. 

__ __ > __ __
__ __ < __ __
__ __ = __ __

F. 

__ __ > __ __
__ __ < __ __
__ __ = __ __

G. 

__ __ __ > __ __ __
__ __ __ < __ __ __

H. 

__ __ __ > __ __ __
__ __ __ < __ __ __

I. 

__ __ __ > __ __ __
__ __ __ < __ __ __

Going Buggy!

Fill in each circle with the correct sign: **<**, **=**, or **>**.

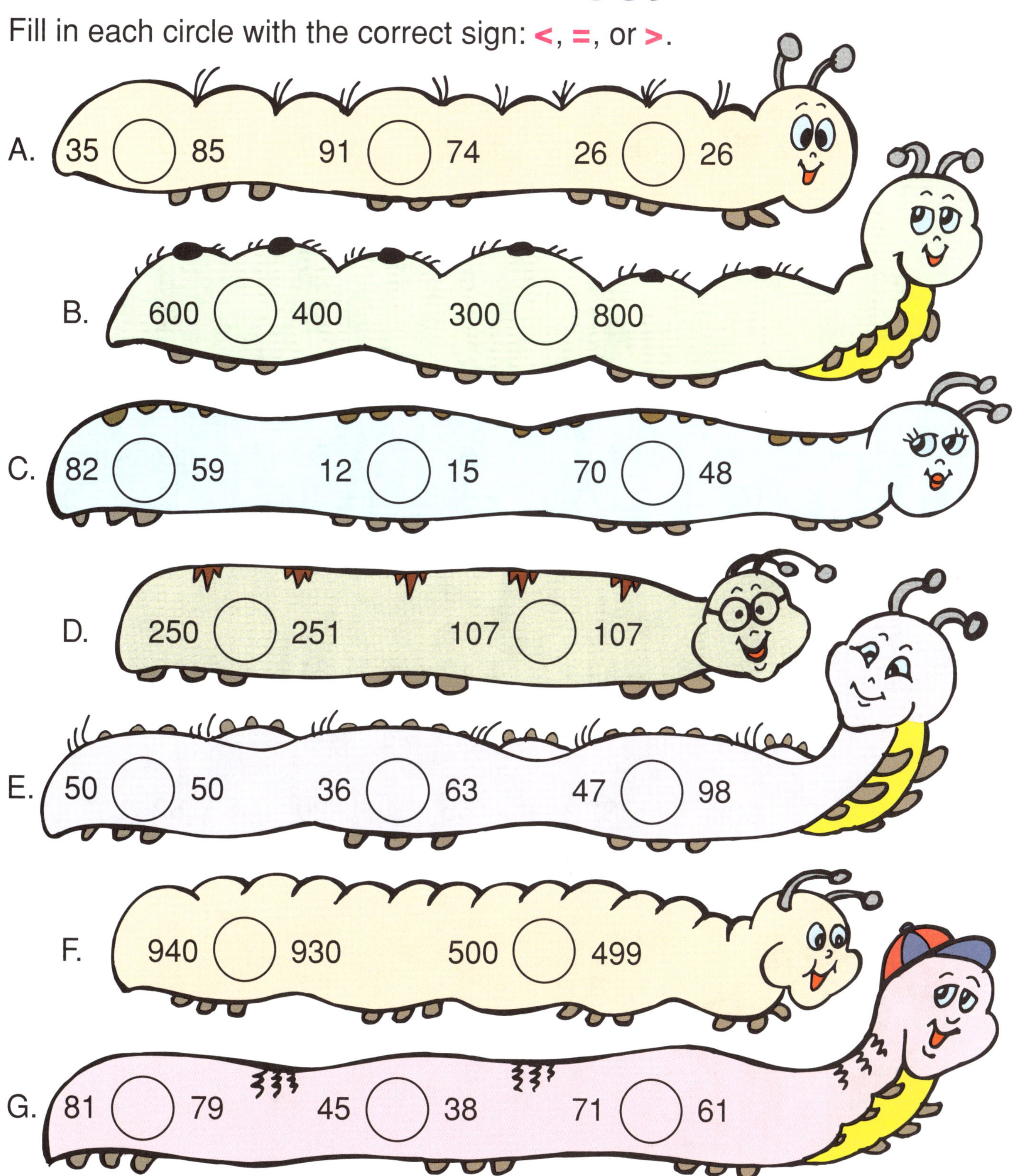

Panda Problems

Add.

A.	65 + 32 97	83 + 11	72 + 26	49 + 50	50 + 35	21 + 71	33 + 46
B.	10 + 52	34 + 34	15 + 41	53 + 30	20 + 24	51 + 46	32 + 43
C.	41 + 57	14 + 63	50 + 27	32 + 40	66 + 21	27 + 11	51 + 30
D.	58 + 41	44 + 55	20 + 59	73 + 12	54 + 31	24 + 40	20 + 63
E.	43 + 53	60 + 31	32 + 47	65 + 23	20 + 40	82 + 11	43 + 55
F.			22 + 75	57 + 42	65 + 14	56 + 33	

Out of This World

Add.

A.

64	40	33	14	26	50	81
+ 25	+ 39	+ 42	+ 71	+ 51	+ 43	+ 15
89						

B.

40	72	65	10	52	53	62
+ 21	+ 27	+ 33	+ 60	+ 41	+ 45	+ 34

C.

67	15	26	56	43	51	57
+ 22	+ 54	+ 73	+ 32	+ 24	+ 43	+ 40

D.

12	29	65	21	43	30	40
+ 76	+ 60	+ 30	+ 21	+ 36	+ 56	+ 42

E.

54	23	40	32	32	51	34
+ 24	+ 60	+ 44	+ 13	+ 62	+ 47	+ 33

F.

72	36	21	71	18
+ 10	+ 51	+ 48	+ 10	+ 80

Shark!

Add.

A.

52	45	39	27	39	53	15
+ 28	+ 26	+ 31	+ 59	+ 38	+ 17	+ 68
80						

B.

28	29	19	13	53	77	23
+ 38	+ 44	+ 25	+ 49	+ 38	+ 13	+ 59

C.

36	68	48	19	78	47	49
+ 59	+ 24	+ 36	+ 59	+ 19	+ 25	+ 24

D.

49	65	24	16	47	32	28
+ 42	+ 25	+ 7	+ 18	+ 28	+ 59	+ 25

E.

39	69	57	58
+ 49	+ 16	+ 36	+ 27

Snowflakes

Add.

A.

34	28	49	59	44	27	75
+ 27	+ 56	+ 25	+ 11	+ 36	+ 58	+ 7

B.

29	86	39	29	38	49	53
+ 69	+ 9	+ 38	+ 24	+ 45	+ 27	+37

C.

36	27	33	28	28	49	53
+ 48	+ 57	+ 18	+ 62	+ 47	+ 42	+ 19

D.

25	64	28	49	28	48	72
+ 18	+ 28	+ 43	+ 13	+ 68	+ 33	+ 18

E.

87	46	64	58	46
+ 5	+ 34	+ 29	+ 37	+ 47

Busy Bats

Subtract.

A. $18 - 9 =$ _____ $14 - 6 =$ _____ $10 - 9 =$ _____

B. $13 - 8 =$ _____ $17 - 8 =$ _____ $14 - 7 =$ _____

C. $14 - 5 =$ _____ $11 - 5 =$ _____ $13 - 4 =$ _____

D. $12 - 4 =$ _____ $16 - 7 =$ _____ $11 - 2 =$ _____

E. $13 - 6 =$ _____ $11 - 4 =$ _____ $10 - 3 =$ _____

F. $15 - 9 =$ _____ $12 - 6 =$ _____ $15 - 7 =$ _____

G.

68	95	78	69	43	77	96
− 25	− 81	− 70	− 57	− 43	− 32	− 4

H.

59	78	53	44	67	89	41
− 56	− 6	− 32	− 20	− 11	− 43	− 11

I.

92	81	66	75	89	32	90
− 22	− 30	− 63	− 42	− 85	− 1	− 10

J.

73	88	59	52	97	88	46
− 61	− 17	− 9	− 40	− 45	− 2	− 30

Subtraction Practice

Subtract.

A. 10 − 4 = ____   11 − 9 = ____   12 − 7 = ____

B. 13 − 5 = ____   16 − 8 = ____   11 − 3 = ____

C. 15 − 8 = ____   14 − 9 = ____   10 − 8 = ____

D. 13 − 9 = ____   12 − 3 = ____   13 − 7 = ____

E. 12 − 6 = ____   10 − 1 = ____   17 − 9 = ____

F. 16 − 9 = ____   11 − 6 = ____   10 − 5 = ____

G.

49	94	67	47	18	87	98
− 10	− 13	− 43	− 21	− 14	− 85	− 40
39						

H.

70	92	96	85	83	45	57
− 20	− 31	− 70	− 10	− 20	− 42	− 34

I.

36	98	87	54	68	36	96
− 31	− 57	− 60	− 40	− 33	− 16	− 95

J.

52	89	57	69	92	19	37
− 10	− 52	− 56	− 24	− 62	− 8	− 27

Rainy-Day Math

Subtract.

A.
$$\begin{array}{r} \overset{8\,15}{\cancel{95}} \\ -\ 38 \\ \hline 57 \end{array}\qquad \begin{array}{r} 70 \\ -\ 64 \\ \hline \end{array}\qquad \begin{array}{r} 51 \\ -\ 29 \\ \hline \end{array}\qquad \begin{array}{r} 82 \\ -\ 67 \\ \hline \end{array}\qquad \begin{array}{r} 43 \\ -\ 5 \\ \hline \end{array}\qquad \begin{array}{r} 96 \\ -\ 68 \\ \hline \end{array}\qquad \begin{array}{r} 61 \\ -\ 43 \\ \hline \end{array}$$

B.
$$\begin{array}{r} 30 \\ -\ 18 \\ \hline \end{array}\qquad \begin{array}{r} 83 \\ -\ 19 \\ \hline \end{array}\qquad \begin{array}{r} 92 \\ -\ 13 \\ \hline \end{array}\qquad \begin{array}{r} 73 \\ -\ 37 \\ \hline \end{array}\qquad \begin{array}{r} 52 \\ -\ 46 \\ \hline \end{array}\qquad \begin{array}{r} 81 \\ -\ 50 \\ \hline \end{array}\qquad \begin{array}{r} 77 \\ -\ 9 \\ \hline \end{array}$$

C.
$$\begin{array}{r} 81 \\ -\ 26 \\ \hline \end{array}\qquad \begin{array}{r} 70 \\ -\ 59 \\ \hline \end{array}\qquad \begin{array}{r} 22 \\ -\ 5 \\ \hline \end{array}\qquad \begin{array}{r} 99 \\ -\ 26 \\ \hline \end{array}\qquad \begin{array}{r} 68 \\ -\ 59 \\ \hline \end{array}\qquad \begin{array}{r} 70 \\ -\ 15 \\ \hline \end{array}\qquad \begin{array}{r} 53 \\ -\ 38 \\ \hline \end{array}$$

D.
$$\begin{array}{r} 61 \\ -\ 7 \\ \hline \end{array}\qquad \begin{array}{r} 94 \\ -\ 27 \\ \hline \end{array}\qquad \begin{array}{r} 84 \\ -\ 75 \\ \hline \end{array}\qquad \begin{array}{r} 41 \\ -\ 15 \\ \hline \end{array}\qquad \begin{array}{r} 73 \\ -\ 24 \\ \hline \end{array}\qquad \begin{array}{r} 62 \\ -\ 34 \\ \hline \end{array}\qquad \begin{array}{r} 36 \\ -\ 27 \\ \hline \end{array}$$

E.
$$\begin{array}{r} 71 \\ -\ 42 \\ \hline \end{array}\qquad \begin{array}{r} 24 \\ -\ 18 \\ \hline \end{array}\qquad \begin{array}{r} 85 \\ -\ 39 \\ \hline \end{array}\qquad \begin{array}{r} 90 \\ -\ 3 \\ \hline \end{array}$$

Brighter Vision Skills Review

At the Pond

Subtract.

A.
```
  5 11
  6̸1̸        52        43        65        84        81        30
- 24      - 19      - 36      - 17      - 26      - 58      -  2
  37
```

B.
```
  90        55        51        80        37        71        61
- 27      -  8      - 33      - 61      - 28      - 16      - 49
```

C.
```
  76        72        60        32        82        92        63
- 38      - 26      - 34      - 15      -  9      - 67      - 58
```

D.
```
  53        77        24        48        93        50        80
- 29      - 59      -  9      - 29      - 17      - 49      - 15
```

E.
```
  82        56        60
- 43      - 29      - 18
```

Dinosaur Dilemmas

Guess and test to solve these problems.

Problem 1—A group of 20 Stegosauruses is made up of adults and babies. There are 6 more adults than babies. How many baby Stegosauruses are there?

Work Space

Answer _______________

Problem 2—There are 23 Triceratops and Apatosauruses munching on leaves. There are 5 fewer Triceratops than Apatosauruses. How many Apatosauruses are there?

Work Space

Answer _______________

Problem 3—There are an equal number of 2-legged dinosaurs and 4-legged dinosaurs standing by a swamp. There are 24 dinosaur legs in all. How many dinosaurs are there?

Work Space

Answer _______________

Monster Time

Draw pictures to solve these problems.

Problem 1—There are 2 monsters. Each monster has 2 heads. Each head has 3 eyes. How many monster eyes are there in all?

Work Space

Answer _________________

Problem 2—A monster likes to wear a shirt and shorts. It has 3 shirts (red, blue, and green) and 2 pairs of shorts (black and yellow). How many different outfits can it make?

Work Space

Answer _________________

Problem 3—Three monsters (Ag, Boo, and Coco) are in a circle. Ag tosses a water balloon to Boo, Boo tosses it to Coco, Coco to Ag, and so on. On the tenth toss, the balloon breaks and splashes the monster who was supposed to catch it. Who got wet?

Work Space

Answer _________________

Line Up

Four children are in a line. Read each set of clues.
Write each child's name on the matching line.

1. _________ 2. _________ 3. _________ 4. _________

Clues

- Ali is between Amy and Andy.
- April is last.
- Amy is only next to Ali.

1. _________ 2. _________ 3. _________ 4. _________

Clues

- Maria and Mimi are in the middle.
- Mike is next to Mimi.
- Matt is not first.

In an Aquarium

There are five crayons.
2 of them are broken.
The matching fraction is ⅖.

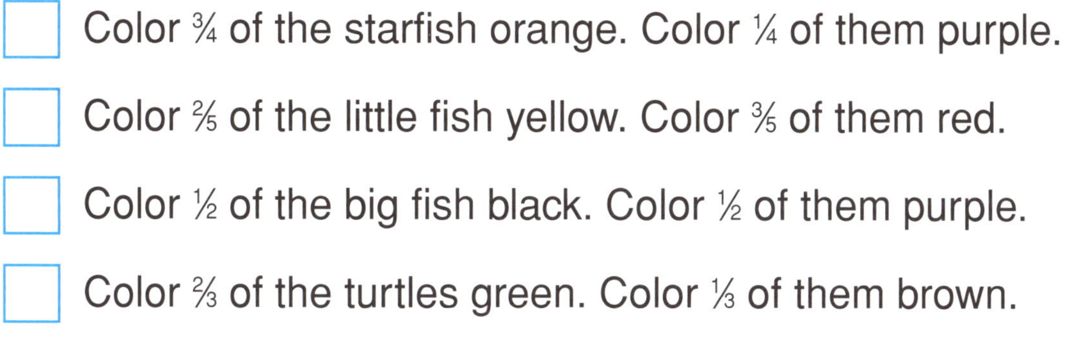

Follow the directions below.

☐ Color ¾ of the starfish orange. Color ¼ of them purple.

☐ Color ⅖ of the little fish yellow. Color ⅗ of them red.

☐ Color ½ of the big fish black. Color ½ of them purple.

☐ Color ⅔ of the turtles green. Color ⅓ of them brown.

☐ Color ¼ of the shells yellow. Leave ¾ of them white.

Flowerbed Fractions

There are 4 presents.
1 of them has a bow.
The matching fraction is ¼.

Follow the directions below.

- [ ] Color ⅚ of the tulips red. Color ⅙ of them yellow.

- [ ] Color ⅔ of the daffodils yellow. Leave ⅓ of them white.

- [ ] Color ¼ of the daisies purple. Color ¾ of them orange.

- [ ] Leave ⅘ of the worms white. Color ⅕ of them yellow.

- [ ] Color ½ of the butterflies orange. Color ½ of them blue.

What Time Is It?

Look at the number for the hour first.
Then count by fives to find the
number of minutes.

12:20
20 minutes after 12 o'clock

Read the clocks. Write the times.

A.  _35_ minutes after _7_ o'clock

_7_ : _35_

B.  _____ minutes after _____ o'clock

_____

C.  _____ minutes after _____ o'clock

_____

D.  _____ minutes after _____ o'clock

_____

E.  _____ minutes after _____ o'clock

_____

Two Kinds of Clocks

Look at the number for the hour first. Then count by fives to find the number of minutes.

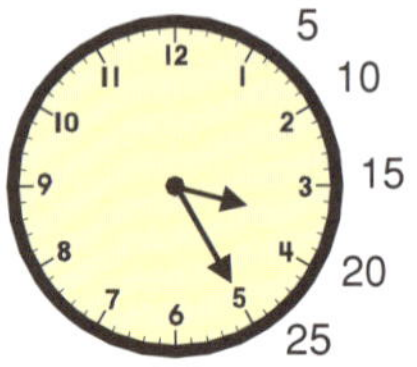

3:25
25 minutes after 3 o'clock

Draw a line from each clock to the clock with the matching time.

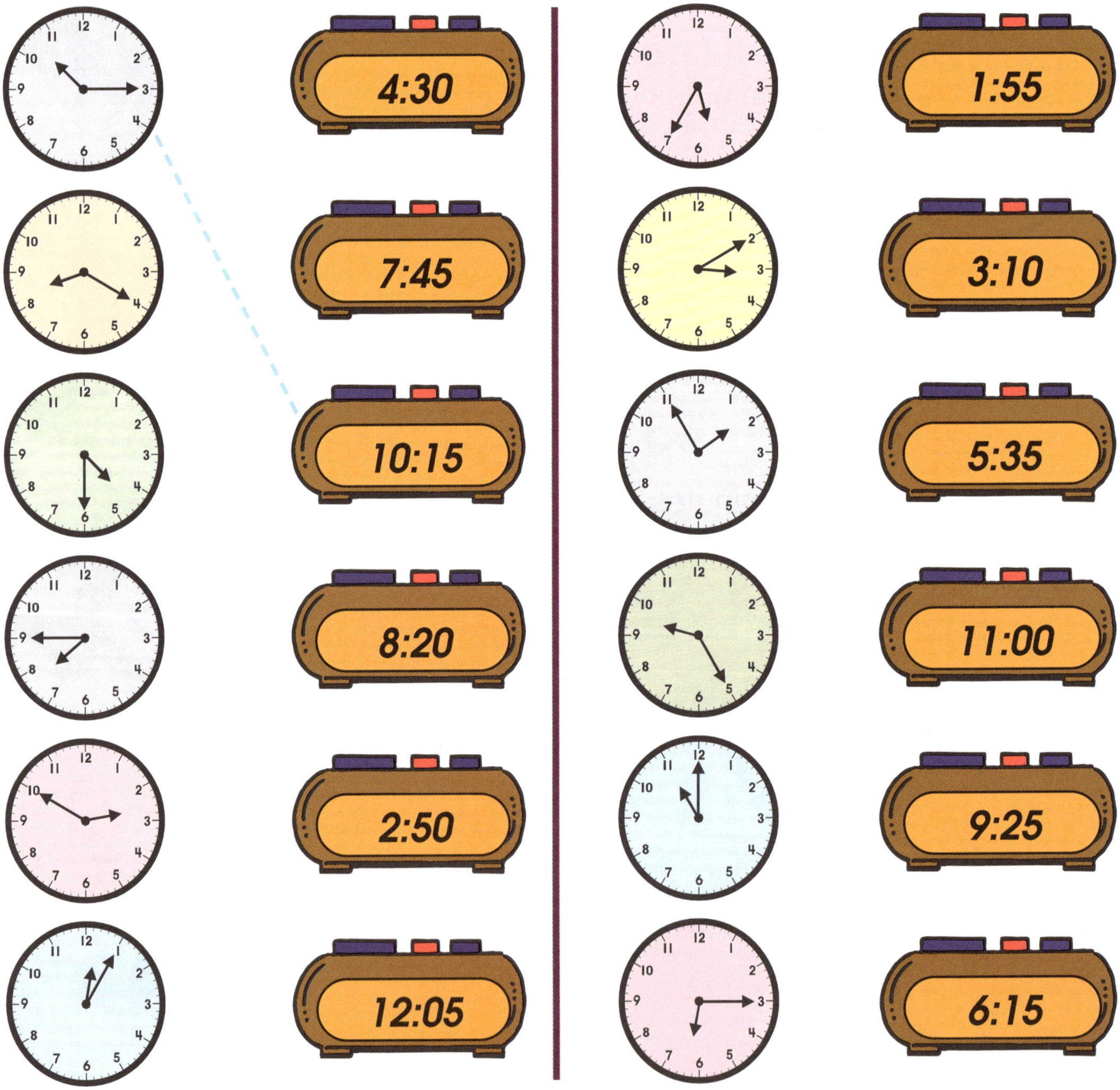

Wonderful Worms

This is a centimeter unit.

This worm is 5 centimeters long.

Choose a worm below.
Estimate its length in centimeters.
Measure it. Record the results on the chart.
Repeat until you have measured each worm.
If you don't have a centimeter ruler, trace the one here.

Worm	Estimated Length	Actual Length
Wavy	cm	cm
Watchful	cm	cm
Wiggly	cm	cm
Wise	cm	cm
Witty	cm	cm
Worried	cm	cm

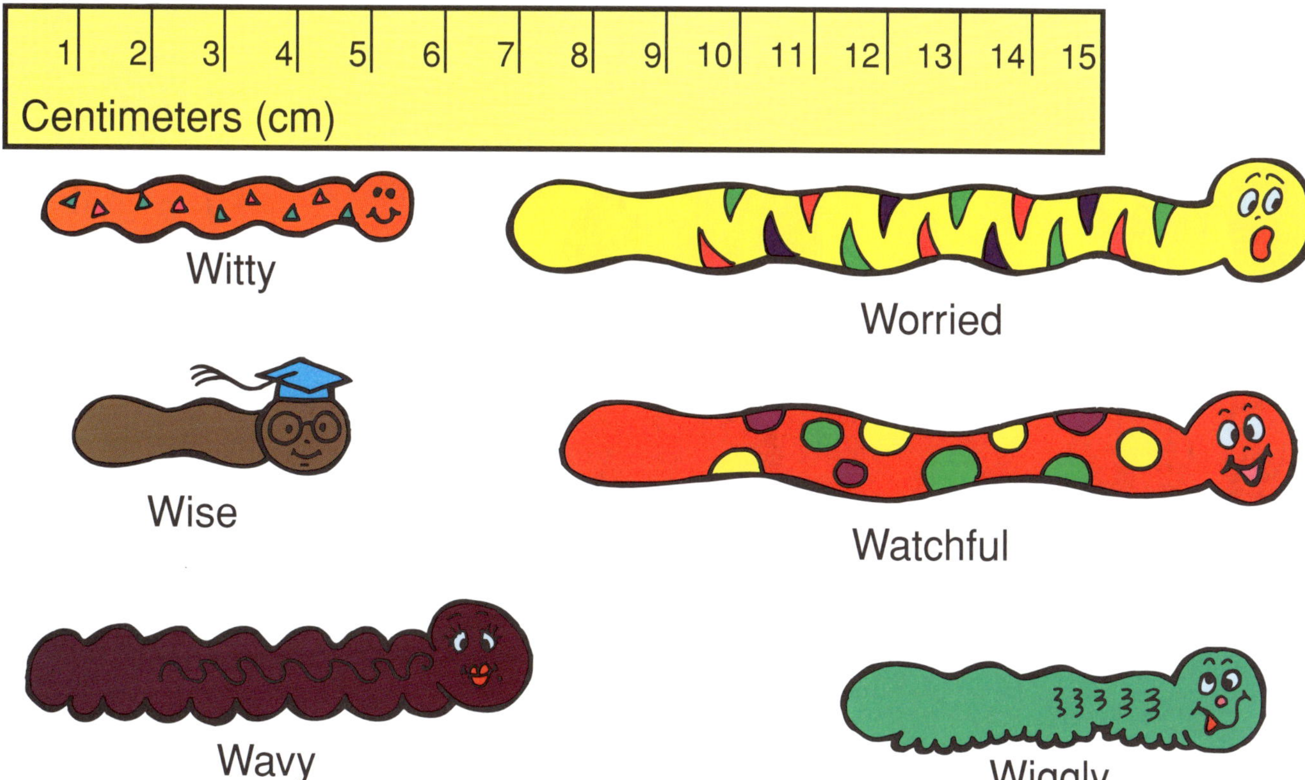

Centimeter Clowns

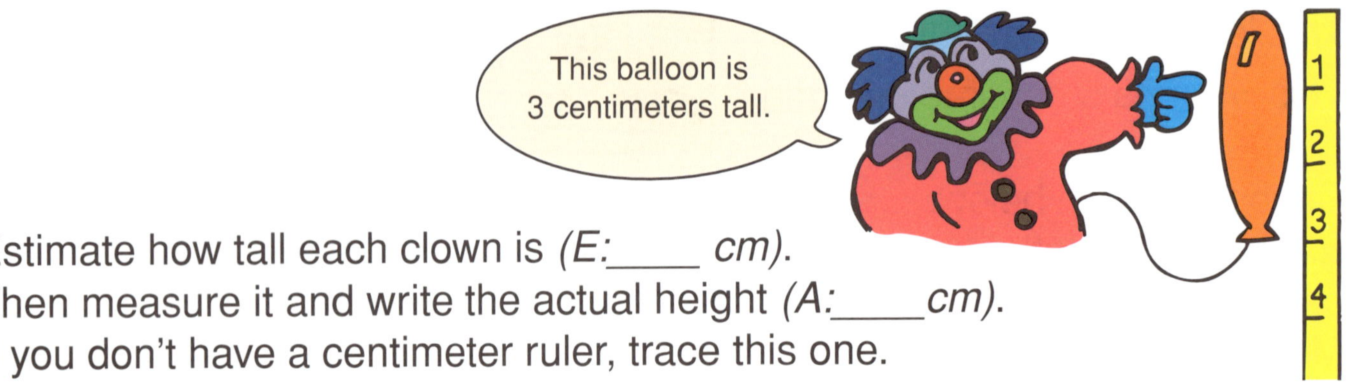

Estimate how tall each clown is *(E:_____ cm)*.
Then measure it and write the actual height *(A:_____cm)*.
If you don't have a centimeter ruler, trace this one.

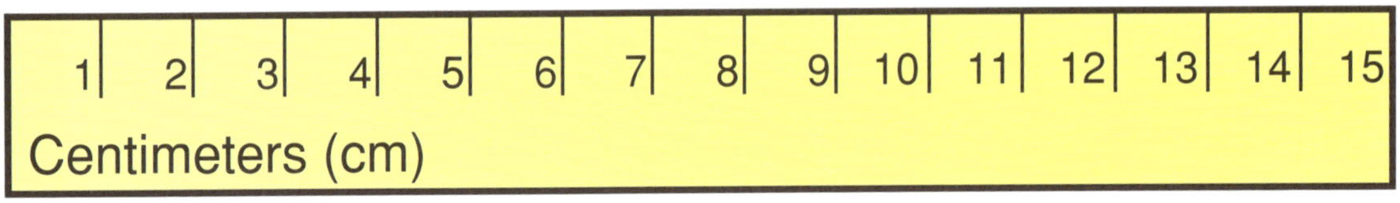

| 1 | 2 | 3 | 4 | 5 | 6 | 7 | 8 | 9 | 10 | 11 | 12 | 13 | 14 | 15 |

Centimeters (cm)

E:_____ cm

A:_____ cm

E:_____ cm

A:_____ cm

E:_____ cm

A:_____ cm

E:_____ cm

A:_____ cm

E:_____ cm

A:_____ cm

Make Your Own Graph

1. Ask 12 people this question: *What is your favorite kind of pizza—cheese, pepperoni, sausage,* or *vegetarian?*

2. Shade in the lowest empty box in the matching column for each answer.

What Is Your Favorite Kind of Pizza?

Cheese   Pepperoni   Sausage   Vegetarian

Answers

Page One

1. me, answer varies
2. snow, answer varies
3. honey, answer varies
4. tail, answer varies
5. break, answer varies
6. chair, answer varies
7. note, answer varies
8. word, answer varies
9. eye, answer varies

Page Two

neigh, play, they
troll, hole, bowl
we, tree, ski
doll, crawl, ball
thumb, some, plum
bread, said, red
fairy, very, cherry
rose, clothes, froze

Page Three

1. story
2. animals
3. start
4. plods
5. sleep
6. noisy
7. reached
8. message

Page Four

1. end
2. Everybody
3. oldest
4. make
5. above
6. find
7. Children
8. wonderful

Page Five

1. be, bee
2. blew, blue
3. two, to
4. whole, hole
5. would, wood
6. I, eye
7. aunt, ant
8. by, buy

Page Six

1, 2, 1, 3, 1, 2, 3, 1, 2, 1

Page Seven

buttercup, butterfly, buttermilk
toothpaste, toothbrush, toothpick
football, basketball, baseball
rowboat, sailboat, tugboat
sunrise, sunflower, sunshine
waterfall, watercolor, watermelon
pancake, cupcake, fruitcake
headlight, flashlight, moonlight

Page Eight

(boy crying)—unhappy, (boy smiling)—happy; (girl saying "Gimme!")—impolite, (girl saying "Please")—polite; (2+2=4)—correct, (2+2=5)—incorrect; (boy lifting barbell)—possible, (baby lifting barbell)—impossible; (boys sharing a cone)—kind, (boy upsetting a cone)—unkind; (hat and tie in midair)—invisible, (boy wearing hat and tie)—visible

Page Nine

dancer, farmer, author
doctor, painter, teacher
plumber, actor, sculptor
The suffixes should be circled.

Page Ten

1. artist
2. born
3. Mexico
4. pictures
5. walls
6. grew
7. huge
8. painted
9. asked
10. working

Page Eleven

1. a thin coat of oil
2. water that seeps into your skin
3. goes into
4. Answer varies.

Page Twelve

1. a kind of deer
2. cold northern areas of North America
3. both males and females have antlers
4. Answer varies.

Page Thirteen

1. a silly poem
2. A grasshopper might step on an elephant's toe. Bananas would grow.
3. An elephant wouldn't cry. An elephant wouldn't really talk.
4. grow and toe, eyes and size

Page Fourteen

Woman Dies From Eating Many Animals
Naughty Rabbit Turned Into Goon

Page Fifteen

A. fawn
B. lioness
C. a male sheep
D. a baby kangaroo
E. elephant and whale
F. deer and kangaroo
G. Answer varies.

Page Sixteen

A. 2
B. 15
C. War Planes
D. Modern Airplanes
E. 6
F. Early attempts at flying

Page Seventeen

Order of words on each pencil may vary.
Long vowels: cake, feet, pipe, mule, soap, sale, cube, be, hope, dime
Short vowels: step, hat, pig, up, mop, job, hill, nut, tap, flag

Page Eighteen

i (blue), a (orange), a (blue), o (orange)
i (orange), e (blue), a (orange), o (orange)
a (blue), a or i (blue), e (blue), e (orange)
u (orange), e (orange), e (blue), a (orange)
o (blue), a or i (blue), i (orange) o (blue)

Page Nineteen

1. March
2. forty
3. purple
4. perfume
5. fern
6. nurse
7. girl
8. farm
9. circus
10. birthday
11. market
12. skirt

Page Twenty

Order of words in each box may vary.
Book: took, hook, good, foot, hood, cook, wood, stood, shook, look
Boot: tool, moon, school, room, tooth, roof, soon, pool, mood, zoo

Page Twenty-one

Cow: town, clown, owl, flower, brown, now, how, down, shower, towel, crown, power
Crow: grow, know, blow, slow, window, snow, show, bowl, tow, below, throw, glow

Page Twenty-two

1. soil
2. voice
3. boy
4. toy
5. coin
6. point
Riddles will vary.

Page Twenty-three

A. 3, 2, 1
B. 3, 1, 2
C. 1, 3, 2
D. 2, 1, 3
E. 1, 2, 3
F. 2, 1, 3
G. 1, 2, 3
H. 2, 3, 1
I. 1, 3, 2
J. 2, 1, 3
K. 3, 1, 2
L. 2, 3, 1

Page Twenty-four

1. didn't
2. she's
3. didn't
4. they're
5. can't
6. he'd
7. we'll
8. who's
9. wouldn't

Page Twenty-five

1. I am
2. does not
3. we are
4. she will
5. could have
6. it is
7. they are
8. let us
9. who is
10. have not
11. here is
12. he would

Page Twenty-six

A. houses
B. inches
C. shells
D. boxes
E. buses
F. lines
G. pens
H. chairs
I. bushes
J. keys
K. foxes
L. dishes

Page Twenty-seven

1. dream
2. aliens
3. bed
4. eyes
5. ear
6. noise
7. stairs
8. answer
9. lights

Page Twenty-eight

play—played
work—worked
go—went
like—liked
swim—swam
fly—flew
talk—talked
sing—sang
call—called
are—were
write—wrote
have—had
make—made
say—said
do—did
see—saw
get—got
take—took
live—lived
know—knew
give—gave
think—thought
tell—told
come—came
want—wanted
show—showed
put—put
read—read
ask—asked
try—tried

Page Twenty-nine

clopped, clops
hopped, hops
crept, creeps
leapt, leaps
stalked, stalks
squawked, squawks

Page Thirty

1. September
2. Rogers
3. It
4. Midnight
5. I
6. Tuesday
7. Dr.
8. Hayes
9. She
10. Hook

Page Thirty-two

1. The Taj Mahal is a famous building.
2. It is in India.
3. The Taj Mahal was built many years ago.
4. It was built to honor a queen who died.

Page Thirty-three

1. The manatee is a mammal.
2. It lives in water.
3. Manatees are endangered for two reasons.
4. Their water is polluted.
5. Motorboats run over manatees and kill them.

Page Thirty-four

1. (!)
2. (?)
3. (.)
4. (?)
5. (.)
6. (.)
7. (?)
8. (.)
9. (.)
10. (?)
11. (.)
12. (. or !)

Page Thirty-five

1. (!)
2. (.)
3. (.)
4. (?)
5. (?)
6. (.)
7. (. or !)
8. (.)
9. (?)
10. (.)
11. (.)
12. (. or !)

Page Thirty-six

1. you
2. was
3. years
4. helped
5. waiting
6. hear
7. phone
8. want
9. said
10. spilled

Page Thirty-seven

1. my
2. know
3. first
4. grade
5. year
6. worry
7. other
8. ready
9. one
10. what

Page Forty-three

2, 1, 4, 3
First, Jack's kitten ran up a tree. Next, Jack asked his mother to help him get the kitten. Then Jack's mom brought the kitten a saucer of milk. Finally, the kitten climbed down to get the milk.

Answers continued

Page Forty-six

Insects: ladybug, grasshopper, ant, butterfly, Answer varies.
Sports: soccer, basketball, ice skating, swimming, Answer varies.
Colors: black, purple, gold, green, Answer varies.
Body Parts: skin, brain, stomach, bones, Answer varies.

Page Forty-seven

Accept reasonable answers. The following are possible answers:
1. sea animals
2. trees
3. instruments
4. planets
5. dairy foods
6. vegetables
7. numbers
8. fruit
9. art things

Page Forty-eight

go, woman, angry, right, begin, noisy, below, less

Page Forty-nine

1. hear
2. seal
3. desert
4. color
5. meow
6. year
7. bounce
8. car
9. poem
10. freeze

Page Fifty

Butterfly: 3, 1, 2, 4
Frog: 2, 4, 1, 3

Page Fifty-one

From left to right: 6, 1, 2, 3, 4, 5

Page Fifty-three

1. He is full. He doesn't feel well.
2. She's scared. She's having a good time.
3. Your teacher is sick. Your teacher is at a day-long meeting.
4. He is hurt. He is sad.

Page Fifty-four

Accept reasonable answers.
1. can't tell; It could be any school day.
2. true; You can see them eating.
3. true; You can see the rain on the umbrella.
4. can't tell; They might be planting flowers.

Page Fifty-six

A. 72, 70, 69, 67, 66, 65, 64
B. 218, 220, 222, 223
C. 40, 45, 55, 60, 70, 75
D. 600, 400, 300, 200
E. 8, 12, 14, 16, 20, 22, 24
F. 93, 87, 85, 83, 79, 75
G. 570, 580, 610, 630
H. 15, 21, 27, 30, 36, 42
I. 51, 61, 71, 91, 111
J. 600, 450, 350
K. 85, 75, 70, 60, 55, 50
L. 39, 50, 60, 69

Page Fifty-seven

A. 86, 88, 89, 90, 92, 93
B. 343, 341, 339, 337
C. 50, 70, 80, 100, 130
D. 85, 70, 65, 55, 50, 45
E. 400, 600, 700, 900,
F. 52, 48, 44, 42, 40, 36
G. 315, 330, 335, 345
H. 710, 690, 660,
I. 7, 11, 13, 17, 21, 27
J. 108, 112, 116, 118
K. 699, 499, 399, 199
L. 20, 32, 40, 56

Page Fifty-nine

A. <, >, =
B. >, <
C. >, <, >
D. <, =
E. =, <, <
F. >, >
G. >, >, >

Page Sixty

A. 97, 94, 98, 99, 85, 92, 79
B. 62, 68, 56, 83, 44, 97, 75
C. 98, 77, 77, 72, 87, 38, 81
D. 99, 99, 79, 85, 85, 64, 83
E. 96, 91, 79, 88, 60, 93, 98
F. 97, 99, 79, 89

Page Sixty-one

A. 89, 79, 75, 85, 77, 93, 96
B. 61, 99, 98, 70, 93, 98, 96
C. 89, 69, 99, 88, 67, 94, 97
D. 88, 89, 95, 42, 79, 86, 82
E. 78, 83, 84, 45, 94, 98, 67
F. 82, 87, 69, 81, 98

Page Sixty-two

A. 80, 71, 70, 86, 77, 70, 83
B. 66, 73, 44, 62, 91, 90, 82
C. 95, 92, 84, 78, 97, 72, 73
D. 91, 90, 31, 34, 75, 91, 53
E. 88, 85, 93, 85

Page Sixty-three

A. 61, 84, 74, 70, 80, 85, 82
B. 98, 95, 77, 53, 83, 76, 90
C. 84, 84, 51, 90, 75, 91, 72
D. 43, 92, 71, 62, 96, 81, 90
E. 92, 80, 93, 95, 93

Page Sixty-four

A. 9, 8, 1
B. 5, 9, 7
C. 9, 6, 9
D. 8, 9, 9
E. 7, 7, 7
F. 6, 6, 8
G. 43, 14, 8, 12, 0, 45, 92
H. 3, 72, 21, 24, 56, 46, 30
I. 70, 51, 3, 33, 4, 31, 80
J. 12, 71, 50, 12, 52, 86, 16

Page Sixty-five

A. 6, 2, 5
B. 8, 8, 8
C. 7, 5, 2
D. 4, 9, 6
E. 6, 9, 8
F. 7, 5, 5
G. 39, 81, 24, 26, 4, 2, 58
H. 50, 61, 26, 75, 63, 3, 23
I. 5, 41, 27, 14, 35, 20, 1
J. 42, 37, 1, 45, 30, 11, 10

Page Sixty-six

A. 57, 6, 22, 15, 38, 28, 18
B. 12, 64, 79, 36, 6, 31, 68
C. 55, 11, 17, 73, 9, 55, 15
D. 54, 67, 9, 26, 49, 28, 9
E. 29, 6, 46, 87

Page Sixty-seven

A. 37, 33, 7, 48, 58, 23, 28
B. 63, 47, 18, 19, 9, 55, 12
C. 38, 46, 26, 17, 73, 25, 5
D. 24, 18, 15, 19, 76, 1, 65
E. 39, 27, 42

Page Sixty-eight

7, 14, 8

Page Sixty-nine

12, 6, Boo

Page Seventy

1. Amy, 2. Ali, 3. Andy, 4. April
1. Mike, 2. Mimi, 3. Maria, 4. Matt

Page Seventy-one

Picture is colored as directed.

Page Seventy-two

Picture is colored as directed.

Page Seventy-three

A. 35, 7, 7:35
B. 15, 9, 9:15
C. 20, 11, 11:20
D. 45, 1, 1:45
E. 30, 4, 4:30

Page Seventy-four

The analog clocks should be matched to the digital clocks with the corresponding times.

Page Seventy-five

Estimated lengths will vary.
Actual lengths: 7, 10, 6, 4, 5, 11

Page Seventy-six

Estimated heights will vary.
Actual heights (from left to right): 10, 4, 8, 6, 9